The All About Series

All About ... Canadian Animals

Canada

Lynxes

Barb McDermott and Gail McKeown
Reidmore Books

Reidmore Books Inc.

18228 - 102 Avenue
Edmonton, AB T5S 1S7
phone (780) 444-0912
toll-free 1-800-661-2859
fax (780) 444-0933

website: http://www.reidmore.com
email: reidmore@compusmart.ab.ca

printed and bound in Canada

©1998 Reidmore Books

Canadian Cataloguing in Publication Data
McDermott, Barb.
All about Canadian animals : lynxes

(All about series)
Includes index.
ISBN 1-896132-21-9

1. Lynx--Canada--Juvenile literature. I. McKeown, Gail. II. Title. III. Series: McDermott, Barb. All about series. QL737.C23M315 1998 j599.75'3'0971 C98-910188-6

About the Authors

Barb McDermott and Gail McKeown are highly experienced kindergarten teachers living in Ontario. Both hold Bachelor of Arts and Bachelor of Education degrees, Early Childhood diplomas, specialist certificates in Primary Education, and have completed qualification courses in Special Education. As well, Gail has a specialist certificate in Reading and Visual Arts, and Barb has one in Guidance.

Credits

Editorial: Leah-Ann Lymer, Scott Woodley
Illustration, design and layout: Bruno Enderlin, David Strand

Photo Credits

Entries are by page number, coded as follows:
T=Top, B=Bottom, L=Left, R=Right
Abbreviations: VU=Visuals Unlimited
Cover and stamp photo
VU/R. Lindholm
Page
1 VU/Leonard Lee Rue III
3 L-VU/R. Lindholm; R-VU/Joe McDonald
5 VU/Joe McDonald
7 VU/R. Lindholm
9 John Luke/Image Network Inc.
11 VU/Tom J. Ulrich
13 John Warden/Image Network Inc.
15 VU/Joe McDonald
17 VU/Beth Davidow
19 VU/Leonard Lee Rue III
21 VU/Joe McDonald
23 R-VU/Joe McDonald; L-VU/Glenn Oliver
25 VU/Joe McDonald
27 VU/Joe McDonald

We have made every effort to identify and credit the sources of all photographs, illustrations, and information used in this book. Reidmore Books appreciates any further information or corrections; acknowledgment will be given in subsequent editions.

Table of Contents

(All about what's in the book)

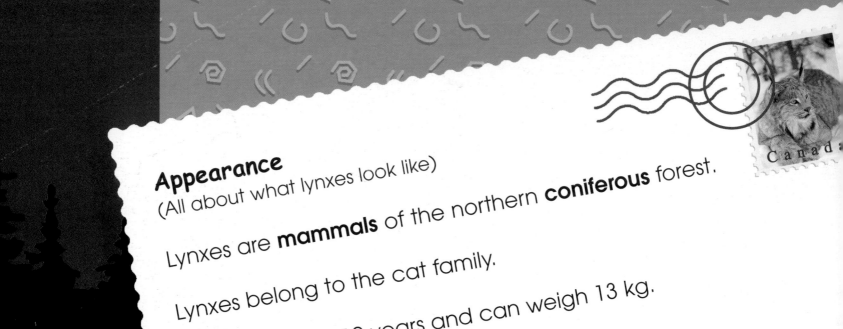

Appearance
(All about what lynxes look like)

Lynxes are **mammals** of the northern **coniferous** forest.

Lynxes belong to the cat family.

Lynxes can live 10 years and can weigh 13 kg.

Lynxes have big, pointy ears and large eyes.

Lynxes have long **tufts** of fur on their ears.

Lynxes have long fur behind their jaws, on their sides, and on their back legs.

Canada

A Lynx

1

Canada

Appearance
(All about what lynxes look like)

Lynxes have 2 fur coats.

Lynxes have brown, spotted fur coats in the summer.

Lynxes have grey, spotted fur coats in the winter.

Lynxes have a short tail with a black tip.

Lynxes have long legs.

Lynxes have big **paws**.

Lynxes can be 90 cm long.

Lynxes Have Long Legs and Big Paws

3

Habitat
(All about where lynxes live)

Lynxes live in the **tundra**.

Lynxes live in the northern forest.

Lynxes live alone.

Lynxes travel a great distance at night.

Lynxes

A Lynx in the Forest

Habitat
(All about where lynxes live)

Lynxes live in a **den**.

Lynxes can build a den under the low branches of a tree.

Lynxes can build a den inside a log.

Lynxes can build a den in a dark, dry cave.

Baby Lynxes in Their Den

Diet
(All about what lynxes eat)

Lynxes are **carnivores**.

Lynxes are **nocturnal**.

Lynxes hunt and eat at night.

Lynxes eat snowshoe hares, mice, squirrels, birds, and caribou calves.

Lynxes eat beavers, foxes, river otters, and muskrats.

A Lynx Catching a Snowshoe Hare

Diet
(All about what lynxes eat)

Lynxes like to eat snowshoe hares in the winter.

Lynxes can eat a snowshoe hare in 1 meal.

Lynxes can eat 150 to 200 snowshoe hares in 1 year.

A Lynx with Its Catch

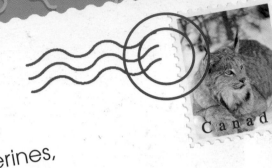

Canada

Predators
(All about the enemies of lynxes)

The enemies of lynxes are wolves, wolverines, and cougars.

Lynxes will climb a tree to **escape** a wolf.

Lynxes are good swimmers.

Lynxes go into the water to escape some enemies.

People can be the enemy of lynxes, too.

A Timber Wolf

Offspring
(All about lynx babies)

Lynx babies are called kittens or cubs.

Kittens are covered with grey fur when they are born.

Kittens drink milk from their mother.

Kittens spend a lot of time playing.

A Lynx Kitten

Offspring
(All about lynx babies)

Lynxes have 1 to 4 babies in the spring.

Lynxes have 1 **litter** every year.

Kittens cannot see or hear when they are born.

Kittens stay in the den until they are 5 months old.

Kittens are fully grown when they are 2 years old.

A Mother and Her Kitten

Adaptation
(All about how lynxes live in their world)

Lynxes have large, padded feet.

Lynxes walk quietly.

Lynx toes are spread apart like a **snowshoe**.

Lynxes travel easily in deep snow.

Lynxes have good eyesight and hearing for hunting.

A Lynx in the Snow

Adaptation
(All about how lynxes live in their world)

Lynxes have **retractable claws**.

Lynxes use their claws for catching **prey**, fighting, and climbing trees.

Lynxes can run fast over a short distance.

Lynxes **stalk** prey that are close by.

Sharp Kitten Claws

21

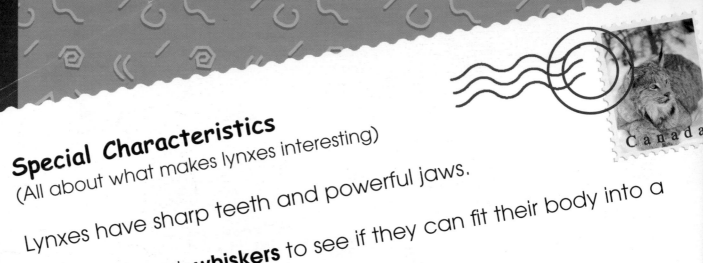

Special Characteristics
(All about what makes lynxes interesting)

Lynxes have sharp teeth and powerful jaws.

Lynxes use their **whiskers** to see if they can fit their body into a small space.

Lynxes have furry feet to keep them warm.

A Lynx Skull

Lynxes Have Sharp Teeth

Special Characteristics
(All about what makes lynxes interesting)

Lynxes are excellent climbers and jumpers.

Lynxes use tall trees for a **lookout**.

Lynxes claw trees to mark their **territory**.

Lynxes Climb Tall Trees

25

Summary

(All about the ending)

Lynxes have long tufts of fur on their ears.

Lynxes are good runners, climbers, and swimmers.

Lynxes are called the "Ghost Cats of the North."

Lynxes are truly amazing animals ... that live in Canada!

Ghost Cat of the North

Glossary
(All about what the words mean)

carnivores (page 8)
Carnivores are animals who eat meat.

claws (page 20)
Claws are sharp nails on the feet of animals.

coniferous (page 1)
Coniferous refers to trees with cones, such as spruce trees and pine trees.

den (page 6)
A den is a place where a wild animal lives.

escape (page 12)
To escape is to get away.

litter (page 16)
A litter is babies born at the same time from the same mother.

lookout (page 24)
A lookout is a place from which to watch.

mammals (page 1)
Mammals are animals who feed their babies milk.

nocturnal (page 8)
Nocturnal means active during the night instead of during the day.

paws (page 2)
Paws are the feet of 4-footed animals with claws.

prey (page 20)
Prey is an animal hunted for food.

retractable (page 20)
Retractable means able to bring back in.

snowshoe (page 18)
A snowshoe is a special shoe for walking on top of the snow.

stalk (page 20)
To stalk is to move towards something without being seen or heard.

territory (page 24)
A territory is an area of land.

tufts (page 1)
Tufts are bunches of soft hair growing from one place.

tundra (page 4)
Tundra is treeless, frozen ground.

whiskers (page 22)
Whiskers are long, stiff hairs growing near the mouth of animals such as a cat.